SPRING TIDES

DRAWINGS BY *Samuel Hanks Bryant*

Spring Tides

by SAMUEL ELIOT MORISON

HOUGHTON MIFFLIN COMPANY BOSTON

The Riverside Press Cambridge

To Priscilla

who has accompanied me
from half flood
to spring full

PREFACE

MY FEELING for the sea is such that writing about it is almost as embarrassing as making a confession of religious faith. Once in a while, however, some incident, view, or scrap of poetry strikes a bell that reverberates through the deeps and brings to the surface impressions and memories extending over many years. When that happens I feel impelled to write something immediately. The chapters that follow have thus been written at various times, generally close to the event, rather than in retrospect.

One gorgeous spring high tide in Maine, when I could sail my boat right up to the trees, suggested the first chapter in this volume; but I could not have completed it but for certain stanzas in St.-John Perse's *Amers (Seamarks)*, which he has kindly allowed me to translate and quote. Spring tides of the spirit, one may say, produced the other chapters: a perfect August day's sail, and Priscilla's superb performance on a September cruise. The chapter on a Yacht's Cabin began when, detained at Matinicus Harbor by a thick-o'-fog, I had time to reflect on the peculiar charm of a snug, well-designed cabin. The resemblance of a tiny harbor on Great Spruce Island in Maine to the sheltered cove described in the first book of the *Æneid* started me rereading the principal Greek and Roman classics to find out what the ancients felt about the sea. Then, in order to see for myself the waters plowed by the row-gallies and sailing ships of the ancients, I gladly accepted an invitation of Alexander Forbes to make a sailing cruise in the Ægean. That was thirty years ago, when his schooner *Ramah* was almost the only yacht in those waters. Impressions of that memorable cruise, jotted down when they were fresh, have been somewhat enlarged after rereading my journal of the voyage.

If you ask why there is no chapter on the Caribbean, the answer is that my West Indies cruises are already woven into three or four books on Columbus, as well as in *By Land and By Sea* which was published twelve years ago. In the book at hand there are no twice-told tales; only fragments on the ancients have previously seen the light of print.

The sea belongs to us all, and every aspect of it from halcyon calm to howling hurricane is fraught with beauty. In these pages I am trying to share with the reader what the sea has meant to me; to pass on to another generation the delight that salt water affords to those who will take the trouble to learn sea lore. To ply, unhurried, the blue deeps, or skirt the shining margents of the land, communing with the element whence life sprang, hearing no other sound but the plash of oar, the flap of sail, the whistling of wind in the rigging, and the swish and gurgle of cloven waves, revives one's strength and refreshes one's spirit. Here the tiniest lad sailing a dinghy becomes partner to the great navigators and discoverers of history; here too, borrowing St.-John Perse's bold metaphor, unity between earth and heaven is recovered, truth is brought to light like the flash of a steel sword blade drawn out of its sheath; and we, the guests, can share the same supper with our Host.

So, hoping that I have not "gone overboard" in presenting these fugitive sketches, I submit them to my readers.

S. E. Morison

Good Hope
Northeast Harbor, Maine
October, 1964

CONTENTS

SPRING TIDES

I. SPRING TIDES

S PRING TIDES are not the tides of spring as many lands-men suppose. They are the very high and very low tides which occur twice a month, with the new and the full moon, when solar and lunar magnetism pull together to make the circumterrestrial tide wave higher than at other times. The opposite to the spring tide is the neap tide, half-way between these phases of the moon; down East, in Maine, there may be as much as five feet difference in range between springs and neaps.

Spring tides are beloved by all who live by or from the sea. At a spring low, rocky ledges and sandbars which you never see ordinarily are bared; the kinds of seaweed that require air but twice a month appear; sand dollars like tarnished pieces of eight are visible on the bottom. Clam specialists can pick up the big "hen" clams or the quahaugs, and with a stiff wire hook deftly flip out of his long burrow the elusive razor clam. Shore birds — sandpiper, plover and curlew — skitter over the sea-vacated flats, piping softly and gorging themselves on the minor forms of life that cling to this seldom-bared shelf.

The rising flood, engendering swift currents, seems determined to overflow the land. St.-John Perse compares the full tides of the new moon to "the rising sea of desire," "when the female land opens to the salacious, supple sea, adorned with bubbles even in its lagoons, its salt marshes, where the sea high in the grass makes a sucking noise, and the night teems with little cracklings." These cracklings (*éclosions*) he calls "the song of bubbles on the sand" — a million little bubbles that the waves deposit, bursting with soft little pops like the soap bubbles that children blow.[1]

A spring high is the time to bathe off sundrenched rocks, or the still dry narrow strip of sand with no stretch of pebbles and shells to hurt your feet. And at a spring high, children row over the furthest stretches of the tide, peering down delightedly at the sea lavender and beach grasses that they usually see well out of water. Curious bits of light flotsam, driftwood in fantastic shapes, green glass net floats, derelict lobsterpot buoys, float up with the spring high and dry out on the shore until some beachcomber picks them up to sell to tourists, or another spring high carries them off. But not all

[1] St.-John Perse *Amers* (*Seamarks*) (New York: Pantheon Books, 1958), p. 102. The author has kindly allowed me to quote him, and to make my own translations.

springs are of equal range. The full moon spring of mid-August, for instance, has a range of 12.5 feet at Portland, Maine; but the mid-October and mid-November ones run to 13.2 feet. By contrast, a July neap in this same harbor ranges barely 6 feet. A northeast gale may build as many as four feet to a spring high, flooding wharves and drowning out cellars near the waterfront. The spring of mid-January 1963 overflowed the bridge to our summer float, lifted it clear of the piers, and carried it out to sea. It also played a joke on local lobstermen by rising so high that their pot buoys were pulled under water. Some busybody ashore, observing waters once dotted with gaily colored pot buoys to be clean as a mirror, jumped to the conclusion that lobster thieves had been cutting warps and notified the police, who called the Coast Guard. By the time the cutter arrived the tide was ebbing and the pot buoys were popping to the surface.

Spring highs, for some scientific reason unknown to me, always come within an hour of noon or of midnight. The herring fishermen are waiting for them, as the little fish are borne by the flood into coves and shoal waters where they can be caught more easily. On a calm summer night, with the brimming tide, the tiny fish leap out of water in unison and fall back, making a sound like that of a sudden shower on a pond. Presently boats appear, with flares; and amid cheery shouts the eager fishermen run "twine," as they call nets, upheld by cork buoys, around that part of the cove where the herring have been heard and seen. This is the stop seine to prevent the fish from escaping seaward when the tide turns and during the hours of ebb.

Hours pass. The Pleiades rise, followed in late summer

by the Dog Star and Orion. The eastern sky grows pale, then red, heralding the sun whose reflection on the quiet water, lightly furred by the dawn offshore breeze, turns it wine-dark, the Homeric color. Now is the moment for action. The fishermen suspend from a dory and attach to the stop seine the pocket or purse seine, like the pendant on a lady's necklace. Between it and the big net is an opening — the gates of the herring's hell. With a clacking of oars against their boats, and splashing and shouts, the fishermen encourage the herring that are foolishly swimming to and fro on the net's shore side to pass through the gate whence there is no return. Sea gull and tern, cognizant of what is going on, gather in flocks and, screaming with joy, snap up and swallow fingerlings as fast as they come to the surface.

By this time a big diesel sardine boat, summoned by telephone, with bags of salt piled on her deck and a weird contraption for scaling herring, is standing by. At the moment judged right by the fishermen, the gate to the purse is closed and herring in silver streams are scooped up by a great dip net from the big boat. If the herring are the right size and the market is good, they are rushed to the factory where they are canned as Maine sardines. Those too big for the can are run through the descaling machine, these scales having a new market with the makers of costume jewelry. The descaled herring in Maine are generally sold for lobster bait; but at Grand Manan or other places in the Provinces they are cured by smoking, packed in wooden boxes and shipped, mostly to the West Indies. You can sometimes buy them in city fish markets, and tasty morsels they are, the best hors d'oeuvre in the world.

Since high water of a spring tide comes at noon or midnight, low water occurs shortly before sunrise and sunset, depending on the season. The October spring low is something I would not miss. After a day of brisk northwest wind the harbor is glassy calm, reflecting sunset clouds, the brilliant maples on the shore, and the white hulls of yachts waiting to be hauled out. Around the edge of the sand flats, well below the blue mussel beds, is a rod-wide belt of eel grass catching its fortnightly chance to breathe plenty of oxygen. Big black-backed gulls walk through the grass with a dignified gait, stalking the tiny crabs and little fishes which normally obtain protection among the grass but are now laid bare to the piercing eye and hungry beak.

My favorite spring high on the rocky Maine coast comes in May. It is an esthetic delight to sail in a gentle breeze close to shore when the shadbush is flinging out its white banners among the dark green spruce, the birches are putting forth leaves of the tenderest green, and the birds are "singing like crazy." Equally beautiful, however, are the spring highs on one of those halcyon days in October, when the blueberry bushes on top of the granite cliffs turn a brilliant crimson and the maple near shore sends up torches of gold and scarlet among the evergreen, all reflected in the quiet waters. No birds sing, but the crickets are lively, and if you sail close to where a meadow touches the shore you can hear a violin concerto of their little *cri-cri*. Lovers of Vermont and other inland states assert that their regions display the world's most brilliant colors in the fall of the year. Perhaps so; for who could test them with a color card? But the maples of Maine and the Maritime Provinces at least seem more brilliant, because of their background of dark green spruce and bright blue sea.

The "salacious, supple sea" nibbles at the land in every spring high. One can observe the change in the shoreline over a series of years. Here a boulder is unbalanced and rolls onto the beach; there a spruce which has hopefully stretched out over the water to gather sunlight, loses its balance when a spring high sucks at its roots, and falls overboard; a clump of birches, undermined by the sea viciously undercutting the sandbank where it has been growing, topples and lies forlornly, roots in air, unless someone cuts it up for firewood. This is why people who love their shoreline build stone sea walls to restrain the robber tide; but if the present trend continues the sea will have its way in the end. Highland Light has had to be moved twice in our time, as the sea bites further and further into the skinny arm of Cape Cod.

Shakespeare has Brutus remark:

> There is a tide in the affairs of men,
> Which, taken at the flood, leads on to fortune.

True enough, as Shakespeare had ample opportunity to observe in London River. There, if a sailing barge "missed its tide" it had to wait twelve hours, half of them sitting miserably on the bottom alongside an odorous dock, to catch another ebb to take her down the Thames. You may still see what the tide can do every day in the Tagus off Lisbon. A fleet of *fragatas,* the sailing lighters, part drifts, part sails up that noble river with the flood. The wind drops, the tide turns, and of a sudden you hear the rattle of forty chain cables off Black Horse Square as every vessel bound upriver anchors to await the next unpredictable fair wind or predictable fair tide.

Their predictability explains why tides are the sailor's friend. With a tide and current table he can figure them out to a minute; and even without modern aids he knows the full-and-change factor for his neighborhood, and has been shown by his grandfather how the currents work. Years ago, struggling with engine against a flood tide current between East Quoddy Head and Cutler, I barely overtook a fisherman who, with no other means of propulsion than sweep and sail, worked the eddies so close to that ironbound coast that he made good progress against the strong tidal current. Shipbuilders loved the spring tide, enabling them to build large vessels on convenient spots, at the very head of tidewater, in their very backyards; yet launch and float them at the top of a spring ebb. At low water, take a look from the head of tide in Kennebunkport, or over Duxbury Bay, now a green meadow of eelgrass, and you can hardly believe that hundreds of tall ships were there built, launched, and sailed or poled down to deep water. At the North River in Massachusetts, ships were built as high upstream as Hanover bridge, launched on a spring high and towed downstream on the ebb; a gang of men with a hawser on each bank, and the pilot, at the knightheads, ordering, "A leetle more over toward Scituate!" or, "Marshfield side, and put more back into it!"

Since tides, like the movements of sun, moon and stars, were phenomena that man could not influence, it was man's natural conclusion that they affected his life. Just as farmers regulated plowing and sowing by the phases of the moon, so sailors and fishermen believed that flood tide meant strength, and ebb tide, weakness. If an old salt lay at death's door, his family and friends watched the tide. If he survived an ebb he would improve with the flood, but he would always die on the ebb. It was a pretty conception that the sailor's spirit would wish to float out of harbor with the ebb and once more survey familiar scenes — kelp-marked ledges, foaming tide rips, circling sea birds, friendly lighthouses — before it left for another world. That this belief was not confined to the coast is attested by Walt Whitman on the Civil War:

"He went out with the tide and the sunset," was a phrase I heard from a surgeon describing an old sailor's death under peculiarly gentle conditions.

During the Secession War, 1863 and '64, visiting the army hospitals around Washington, I formed the habit and continued it to the end, whenever the ebb or flood tide began the latter part of day, of punctually visiting those at that time populous wards of suffering men. Somehow (or I thought so) the effect of the hour was palpable. The badly wounded would get some ease and would like to talk a little or be talked to. Intellectual and emotional natures would be at their best; deaths were always easier; medicines seemed to have better effect when given then; and a lulling atmosphere would pervade the wards.

Similar influences, similar circumstances and hours, day-close, after great battles, even with all their horrors. I had more than once the same experiences on the fields covered with the fallen or dead.[2]

Something of the same feeling comes over every lover of the sea at the turn of a spring tide, especially if the wind is offshore. His soul seems to be pulling his body seaward. He feels an almost irresistible impulse to knock off whatever he may be doing, launch the punt, row out to his sail or motor boat, make sail or start the engine, and speed out into blue water with the ebb, which on a spring tide will carry him through the narrow channel with unusual speed. Around sunset, when the tide turns, he can point his prow home once more, and feel the ineffable delight of half-sailing, half drifting to his mooring with the lightest of sea breezes, under a full moon; or in the new-moon spring, under stars that have guided mariners for thousands of years.

[2] Quoted from *Walt Whitman's Civil War*, edited by Walter Lowenfels (Alfred A. Knopf, Inc., 1961), p. 111. Used by permission of Alfred A. Knopf, Inc., New York.

II. A YACHT'S CABIN

WHY IS a small sailing yacht's cabin so altogether delightful to boys? It certainly is no luxury. The cabin of any sailboat from twenty to thirty feet long used to be highly uncomfortable, by land standards. In my youth, the fashion of yacht design never gave one headroom below, that is, room to stand up, except in really big yachts. To avoid bumping your head you had to walk about the cabin in a crouch, or sit on the transoms which did duty for seats by day and bunks by night. The table was usually a folding contraption which had a way of collapsing whenever someone's toe or knee struck a leg. The stove, usually a one- or two-burner oil gadget that had to be primed with alcohol and pumped violently to burn, gave out little heat and was difficult to cook a square meal on. The toilet, if it was some-

thing more than a chamber pot under a seat up forward,
seldom worked beyond the first week after leaving the yard.
In every rain, water found little cracks in the deck or the
house to drip through, so that one had to spread a poncho
over one's blankets to keep reasonably dry. Water also ran
down the mast into the cabin and dripped in through the
companionway when the tide swung your boat stern to wind.
There was a distinct smell to a small yacht's cabin — com-
posed of dampness, oil clothing, sweaters, underclothes and
dirty dishcloths, with overtones of whatever had been spilled
from the last meal.

Yet there was nothing so fascinating to a youngster as one
of those moldy, cramped, confined cabins. Lads loved cruising as much for cooking meals below and sleeping in damp
blankets as for the sailing and visiting strange coasts and
harbors. Boys begged to be allowed to sleep on board a small
yacht in harbor rather than a comfortable bedroom ashore.
Children who threw their belongings about at home readily
submitted to the yacht discipline that everything must be
put back; and boys finicky about their food ate with gusto
doubtful concoctions out of cans, or the fish that they caught
from the cockpit.

Possibly this love for a small cabin was atavistic, derived
from our remote ancestors for whom a cave was the only safe,
indeed the only possible dwelling. Whatever the origin, it was
part of a yearning for something compact, small, closed-in
from the world. For the same reason probably, children love
small playhouses or snow igloos. At the northern New England school that I attended, three of us constructed a snow
igloo in the deep woods. It was entered on all fours through

an elaborate tunnel which was supposed to confound any nosy schoolmaster who might take it into his head to follow our snowshoe tracks; for we also had a second exit through which we could escape while the master was involved in the snail-like wanderings of the tunnel. Once inside you found a conical room of hardpacked snow, strewn with hemlock and pine boughs which made comfortable sitting. A spirit lamp was kept in a little niche with a tiny chimney. Of an afternoon we cooked the forbidden hot-dog while smoking the forbidden cigarette, and even reading some forbidden novel like Daudet's *Sappho*. This pleasure passed with the first spring thaw; and when in spring term we visited the spot where the igloo had stood and found nought but yellowed hemlock needles and rusty cans to mark it, we had a feeling like Aeneas's sigh over the desolate site of Troy.

All this feeling for the hut, igloo or cabin might be put down to a mere male counterpart to little girls' love for dollhouses and playing house, if the boys ever grew out of it; but they don't. Look at the submariners. People wonder why sailors enjoy being shut under hatches for days — and now for months on end; but they love it. The submarine service is the most popular branch of the Navy, although the most dangerous; and it attracts some of the best men. One reason is the close human association. You really get to know a man in the same submarine, as boys make lifetime friends from shipmates on a cruise in a tiny sailboat. But there is something more to it than that. Your submarine, like your yacht cabin, is shut off from the outside world and all its problems. It is a little world in itself. Everything is in place. Everyone knows what to do in an emergency, and each man knows that

every other shipmate knows what to do. Besides, you are in a sense an explorer, a pioneer, a successor to Champlain or Captain John Smith.

Maybe there is an even more subtle reason for our love of a yacht — the parallel of a well-built hull with a fair woman's body. St.-John Perse suggests this in his *Sea Marks:* "Slender are the vessels, and more slender still thy figure, O faithful body of my beloved. . . . And what is this body itself but the image and form of the ship? — boat, ship and votive model, even to its 'midships opening, built like a vessel's frame, fashioned on her curves, bending the double arc of ivory to the will of sea-born curves. . . . Shipbuilders of every era have used this fashion to bind the keel to the play of knees and frames."[1]

These members, revealed in a proper yacht cabin, are part

[1] St.-John Perse *Amers (Seamarks)* (New York: Pantheon Books, 1958), p. 103.

of its charm. The keel, of course, is hidden by the cabin sole, but the frames, rising from the keel into which they are nicely mortised, may be glimpsed at their upper ends. They appear in the gap between ceiling (sheathing to you) and the top carling or clamp — the fore-and-aft member directly under the deck. If you don't leave this air space you invite dry rot; but it is also a convenient place for mosquitoes to hide during the day and sortie by night to make a meal off the sleeping crew. Also visible are the knees, fashioned from the natural crooks of an oak tree, which strengthen the vessel's hull. The cabin house, which must be built like a flattish dome to shed water at all angles, is strengthened by thwart-ship deck beams, or half-beams when interrupted by a skylight. Bunks tuck in neatly under the deck outside the cabin house, so that room is left to circulate in the middle; and drawers are fitted under these bunks to hold your clothes, tools and sundry nuts, bolts and shackles. It is so cozy lying and sleeping in these tucked-in bunks that old sailors have been known to build their beds at home just so, with a "deck" on which the rain patters, bunk boards so they can't roll out if the house gets lively, and screw-tight portholes to see out of. But nobody has found a substitute for the sweet chuckling of water like the laughter of young girls, that you hear outside the hull while lying in a small yacht's bunk.

The forepeak, where functionalism is supreme, is the best part of a cabin for a young boy. Here the mast comes through the deck in a snug fit of partners, the pieces that are supposed to prevent water dripping through. Overhead are the heavy lodging knees forward of the mast, and the bosom knees abaft it. A musty smell of imperfectly dried anchor rode is in the air. Many recent yacht designs, especially of motor cruisers, conceal every functional member with elaborate sheathing so as to make the cabin look like a cocktail lounge or a duplex apartment bedroom. None of that for me!

The amenities of a yacht cabin have been vastly improved in recent years; and this I credit to the women. Sixty years ago no young lady thought of cruising except in a big yacht with paid hands, private stateroom and all that. But around 1912 girls began demanding to do everything their brothers did, and young wives refused to stay at home when their husbands went cruising. The male sex discovered that females not only helped navigate the yacht but kept her neat and clean below and made up bunks nicely with sheets, replacing the unseemly huddle of blankets that came apart in the night. The girls demanded better toilet facilities and got them, soft watertight mattresses instead of the old "donkey's breakfast" that soaked up water like a sponge, new and shiny cooking pots instead of castoffs from the home kitchen, disposable paper plates, towels, and the like. Above all, yacht designers learned from the fishermen to install a real stove, burning coal, wood or charcoal briquettes, to keep the cabin cozy in down-East waters, and to hang lockers near enough the stove to dry out oilskins and soggy clothing. Some genius invented the "scrap trap" — a folding device from which a disposable garbage bag is hung, to replace the old swill cans that capsized in a breeze and never really got clean. But this "modern improvement," "all the comforts of home" business, is often overdone, especially in the cabins of motor cruisers. Air conditioning is an abomination in a yacht cabin. A cruising yacht's cabin ought to be stuffy at night in northern waters. You want it that way after fighting the wind and the sea and maybe getting drenched by salt spray. And in the tropics or the Mediterranean, if you can't sleep in a confined place without air circulation, you should rig a wind sail that will carry the sweet tradewind down to you, or sleep on deck under the stars.

My father, who was dedicated to camping in the Maine woods, never cared much for sailing; but he did take a couple of cruises with me in my engineless 21-footer. He admitted that we had it all over camping in one respect — you did not have to tote your gear from place to place, and so were not limited as to blankets and utensils. We could sleep warm, protected from insect life by screens, and were not limited to one frying pan for cooking. Father missed the campfire, of course; but for me a perfect substitute is the odor of smoke from the Charley Noble (chimney to you) when you start a fire in the shipmate stove with bits of driftwood. Neither spruce bough nor birch twig has the delicious, spicy odor of smoke from a fire made of fragments of an old, brine-soaked lobster trap found cast up on the shore, mixed with hardwood chunks from a carpenter shop.

There is always something to do in a yacht's cabin when snugged down at anchor in a rainstorm or detained in port by thick o' fog. Cleaning, of course; lines to be spliced, hooks to be screwed into beams and bulkheads so that every piece of gear has its place; knives to be sharpened; corrections to be entered in charts; meals like breadstuffs and beans that take long preparation. I always take a few books along, but never seem to find time to read on board. If you can't stay happy on board a small boat in foul weather, you are no sailor.

Two features of yacht design that contribute most to comfort are headroom and beam. Paraphrasing Longfellow I could say, "Build her beamy, O worthy Master!" For you need beam to be uncrowded on deck as well as below; and you need headroom to stand up, dress, wash and cook. Fashions in this respect are always changing as the racing rules are altered. In the 1890's the rules favored great depth of hull, which gave plenty of headroom below, but a very narrow beam. I remember the Tweeds' cutter *Shona,* designed by the famous Fife, which was 42 foot long and only five foot beam; it was said that a sailor looking aloft from the deck was apt to fall overboard if he took a step backward. Yachts of that vintage were so deep in the hull that they required no cabin house to give headroom. They had beautiful flush decks, broken only by cabin skylights and holystoned by the paid hands first thing every morning, to the disgust of sleeping guests. There was often no cockpit; the helmsman stood completely in the open, intercepting plenty of spray; and the crew, unprotected by bulwarks or lifelines, had to watch their footing very carefully indeed.

Next came a new set of racing rules based largely on waterline length, which favored deep fin keels, tremendous overhang of bow and stern, and a hull like a flat canoe. These yachts had plenty of beam but little headroom. Laurence Percival's *Sally VII*, designed by the great Lawley and built in 1903, measured 25 foot waterline but 58 foot overall, with 11-foot beam, 7-foot draft and an enormous sail area. She killed the Massachusetts Bay 25-foot class by her superior speed, but she had a cabin like a shallow tunnel; you couldn't stand up anywhere below, although there were four or five bunks to each side. But how *Sally VII* could sail! My little 21-foot *Clarice* was once passed by her off Frenchmans Bay, both yachts going down East; we only made Cape Split that evening, but she reached St. Andrews.

Gus Loring's 25-footer *Jingo,* though 40 foot over all, had only two bunks plus a pipe berth for "the kid," a very dirty, lazy boy whom old Mr. Loring paid to go along under the erroneous impression that he would prove a help. When I cruised with Gus and his shipmate "Beany" Burnham in *Jingo,* I had to stretch out on the cabin floor. This had its inconveniences, as "Beany" had a habit of waking up in the middle of the night and crying, "Let's go swimming!" Upon which he, Gus and the kid raced over my prostrate body to be first in the icy water. But this ritual was comfortably followed by a hot mug-up of cocoa or coffee; we never carried spirits in those days.

My 22-foot waterline, 40-foot overall sloop *Mariposa,* built around 1911–12 on the same system, had a beautiful little main cabin for two, and one could stand erect under the skylight; but the galley, installed in the overhang, had less than four foot headroom, and to cook on the tiny stove one had to sit on the floor. Boats like this, with keel extending only one-third the overall length, pounded like a PT boat in rough water and then started to leak — and how they could leak! One old crate of this type, incautiously chartered by me for a September cruise, opened up so wide on Petit Manan bar that a bucket brigade of two could hardly keep her afloat until we reached quiet waters, when the water in the cabin was up to the bunks. That cabin was decidedly *not* cozy the following night, and we never did get it completely dry.

A new set of racing rules around 1910 penalized the long overhang and produced a much more wholesome type of yacht. My yawl *Idler,* designed by Sam Crocker and built by Willis Reid in 1927, measured 23 foot waterline, but only 30 overall. Nevertheless, she had full headroom, three good bunks, and a galley where the cook could stand up. By no means as fast as *Mariposa,* she could go places like crossing the Bay of Fundy, where I would not have dared sail a yacht with a long overhang.

Again beam entered into the racing equation, and to meet this (or, some would say, beat it), Sparkman & Stephens designed a fleet of ocean racers, starting with the famous *Dorade* of 1930 — 52 foot 6 inches long, 10 foot 3 inches beam, 8 foot 4 inches draft — which were very fast and seaworthy but most uncomfortable below. I sailed to the West Indies in one of this type, yawl *Ptarmigan,* in the winter of 1937. Her two cabins and galley were commodious, and she was a magnificent sea boat, but a terrific roller and pitcher and thrower of spray in any kind of breeze.

From around 1905, few cruising sailboats were built without auxiliary power, either gasoline or diesel. Designers learned to install an engine under the cockpit where it could be sealed off from the main cabin. An engine not only enabled the limited-time cruiser to make his desired port in a calm; with increasing power it has almost eliminated beating to windward. Nothing has ever been invented to prevent gasoline from becoming a fire hazard afloat, but the diesel engine, heavier and noisier than a gasoline one of corresponding power, does away with that. From the batteries' self-starter one obtains electric current for cabin lamps and running lights; no longer does the junior member of the crew have to fill with kerosene and trim the red and green running lights, or witness the mortification of their going out in the first puff of wind.

Joshua Slocum's famous sloop *Spray,* in which he sailed alone around the world in the 1890's without benefit of power, was 36 foot 9 inches long overall, and 14 foot 2 inches beam; but her hold depth was only 4 foot 2 inches, so the skipper had no headroom in his tiny cabin. My former yawl

Emily Marshall, designed by Sam Crocker in 1945, is only inches shorter than Spray and has 15 inches less beam; but, through providing a deep hold, Crocker managed to afford headroom to a six-footer even in the fore cabin.

The "doghouse," dignified by the name "coach house" on the big old yachts from which it was adopted, is a sort of halfway cabin between cockpit and main cabin. Its deck is only a few feet below the cockpit deck, and a short glassed-in house covers it, rising above the main cabin house. The doghouse is an excellent place to sit in foul weather, and on the bigger yachts it provides two extra bunks for the watch and a small charcoal stove for warmth. I don't know what we would have done without the doghouse of *Ptarmigan* in our winter voyage to the West Indies, where we weathered two near-hurricanes. But, having become the fashion, doghouses are now absurdly provided for every sailing yacht over seventeen foot long thus spoiling the line of the deck and hindering her sailing qualities.

The dog house was also a valued feature of a yacht dear to my heart, ketch *Mary Otis,* owned and partly designed by my late friend and shipmate William D. Stevens. Thirty-five foot waterline, 45 foot overall and 11 foot six inches beam, she had a peculiar cabin arrangement which allowed for a flush deck fore and aft, wonderful for handling sails in a rough sea. The four-cylinder engine and tanks were installed in the center, leaving a passage connecting the two cabins — forward one with two bunks and the galley, after one with two bunks and head. This was ideal for four men ocean-cruising, as *Mary Otis* frequently did, making four Atlantic crossings under her original owner, and a voyage through the Bahamas and around Cuba as part of my Harvard Columbus Expedition. Well ventilated and completely screened, her two little cabins afforded us cool and comfortable nights sailing in the trades; and, later, the shipmate stove suffused its welcome warmth even to the after cabin when we cruised to Nova Scotia.

After several very rough days at sea in *Mary Otis,* the cabin became a sort of refuge from the elements on deck. It reminded me of the "isolated subterraneousness" of Captain Ahab's cabin in *Moby Dick.* Melville is the only writer, to my knowledge, who has observed the "humming silence" which reigns in a cabin, though "hooped round by all the roar of the elements," as a storm abates. That exactly describes it. Snug below, with the scuttle closed, you hear only a continuous humming, a synthesis of wind, waves and creak of rigging, but all else is silence.

The design of almost every sailing yacht over 30 foot long, prior to 1910, was based on the assumption that the owner would employ one or more paid hands, who were provided with folding pipe berths under the forepeak, with no more room than that afforded to a World War II submariner. With the growth of amateur cruising by married couples with children, and the scarcity, enormous wages and cussedness of paid hands, these accommodations, if they could so be called, have been eliminated. The forepeak is devoted to cables and light sails in bags, and a neat little forecabin is provided between forepeak and main cabin. The popular position for the galley is right under the companionway where the amateur cook can exchange insults with the crew topside and hand his concoctions up to the cockpit without loss of heat. The trouble here is that the cook cannot be stopped from using the companionway ladder steps as shelves, which always creates unpleasantness. For my part, I prefer a central galley where the shipmate stove dries and warms the whole cabin in the foggy weather that we generally encounter down East. Nowadays the central galley is often supplemented by a miniature barbecue outfit in the cockpit, over which a meal may be cooked while the yacht is at anchor, and the owner can pretend that he is at home in his own backyard.

Two innovations of recent years have greatly enhanced cabin comfort. One was first made in the ocean racer *Finisterre,* designed by Sparkman & Stephens for Carleton Mitchell of Annapolis. Her dimensions are 27 foot 6 inches waterline, 38 foot 6 inches overall, and 11 foot beam; but she draws one inch less than 4 feet. Her unusually wide beam and small depth of hull are made possible by a new type of bronze centerboard raised and lowered by power. Mr. Mitchell introduced *Finisterre* to an admiring world by winning a Bermuda race, and she has won transatlantic races since; yet she is said to be comfortable below, owing to the ratio of beam to length. She has also brought back into fashion the centerboard, which had been banished from seagoing yachts since the 1880's, when fatal accidents from capsizing caused them to be considered dangerous. The centerboard has always held its own for very small yachts, especially catboats, and the centerboard trunk does not much impair the comfort of a small yacht cabin, as the leaves of the table can be hinged to it.

The other innovation in design is the reverse-sheer sailboat, built of plywood or fiber glass so that beams and knees are eliminated, and with the greatest height of deck and depth of cabin about halfway between bow and stern. Opinions vary as to the seaworthiness of the reverse-sheer plywood boats; I for one would not care to trust myself in one far off shore. But they are very light in weight, so fast in gentle breezes, and pack a surprising amount of space in the cabin. Reverse-sheer yachts with bunks for four people can even be carried on trailers from port to port, enabling the owner to sample waters all the way from Nova Scotia to Texas, or from Vancouver Island to Mexico.

In comparison with the small-yacht cabins of my boyhood — damp, smelly, leaky and uncomfortable, lit by a kerosene lamp — the twenty-five- to thirty-foot sailing yacht of today has many improvements that add to the comfort of sailing without detracting from its joys. The principal ones are auxiliary power, electric lights, bottled-gas stoves, and an electric refrigerator which, now that block ice is hard to come by, has become almost a necessity for people who must have ice for their drinks.

Hundreds of young couples today, accompanied by small children who learn seamanship the right way, are sailing themselves from port to port in these modern small yachts. I wish that hundreds more of those couples whom you see motoring today, the back of their car full of bored, snarling children, would take to cruising by sail instead. For on board a sailboat there is always something to do for every child bigger than a toddler — and the toddler loves to throw things overboard just to hear the splash. There is nothing that knits a family better than cruising; but don't force the kid who does not take to it. And the cruise must be in a sailboat; in a motor cruiser there is no more for a child to do than in a car, and he gets just as bored. And I advise all young cruisers to anchor properly in a harbor, not tie up at a "marina," the yachtsmen's slum.

Thus a small yacht's cabin is not only a home away from home and a floating camp; it is a little, closed-in world where you are free from all anxieties, problems and considerations except the primitive ones of keeping dry, warm and well fed. It is a little space walled off just for you and your ship-mates, and into which you retire after enjoying a day of the most divine form of movement ever invented by man — that of a sailing ship over the ocean. And what more restful sleep than to slip into a bunk while sailing in blue water after a tough watch offshore, and be lulled to sleep in a silence broken only by the rippling, gurgling laughter of the water as the good vessel slips along on her course?

So, I conclude this homily with another quotation from St.-John Perse, my favorite poet of the sea:

> Narrow are the vessels, narrow our couch. Vast is the spread of waters, but wider still our domain in the closed chambers of desire. . . . Love ships, O lovers; love the tide rising high in the chambers of the sea. . . . May this vast dawn called the sea (chosen wings, levy of arms), be ever at our gates; love and sea of the same bed; love and sea in the same bed.

III. AN AUGUST DAY'S SAIL

A LIGHT, caressing southerly breeze is blowing; just
enough to heel the yawl and give her momentum.
The boy and I get under way from the mooring by the usual
ritual. I take in the ensign, hoist the mizzen, cast off main
sheet and slack the backstays; he helps me hoist the mainsail,
sway the halyards and neatly coil them. I take the wheel and
the main sheet in hand, the boy casts off the mooring rode
and hoists the jib, and off she goes like a lively dog let off
the leash.

We make a long, leisurely beat to windward out of the
Western Way, with tide almost dead low; the reefs, sprayed
with brown rockweed, show up clearly. We pass the bell
buoy and leave to starboard the naked reef known to proper
chart makers as South Bunkers Ledge, but to Mount De-
serters as "Bunker's Whore."

Now we are in the open sea, nothing between us and Nova Scotia. The day is pleasantly cool and bright, with gathering cirrus clouds that sometimes obscure the sun. Old ocean today is green, heaving with a surge farflung from a blow somewhere between us and Europe. Visibility is so high that the horizon is a clean-cut line over which one can see the masts of fishing draggers whose hulls are concealed by the earth's bulge. Seaward, the Duck Islands seem to float on the emerald waters. Landward, the rocky shores of Great Cranberry Island are misty with the spray from a line of white breakers. One thinks of Heredia's line about Britanny: "Du Raz jusqu'à Penmarc'h la côte entière fume" — the entire coast is smoky. Ocean swell makes the yawl roll and pitch, not unpleasantly but in harmonious cadence with the sea, the motion starting little snaps and whistles among the cordage, and the tapping of reef-points on the mainsail.

This is the time for the lunch that Priscilla prepared for us — jellied eggs and baby carrots as hors d'oeuvres; mushroom soup in a thermos; succulent ham sandwiches freshly made with lettuce and mayonnaise; chilled beer from the icebox; homemade doughnuts, crisp outside and flaky-soft inside, as you find them only when made by a master hand in Maine.

Now we are off Bakers Island where the long, flat granite ledges, washed clean by winter gales, hang over a reddish-brown apron of kelp and dulse, whirling in the breakers that roar in past the Thumper ledge. We round the groaner, the perpetually whistling buoy, haul our wind and turn northward.

Here we face the superb panorama of Mount Desert Island

and Frenchmans Bay. The westering sun kindles the granite summits of Sargent, Green and Newport mountains to rose color; and the ocean between us and them is cobalt blue. Spruce-dark Otter Cliff and bare, brown Great Head thrust out into Frenchmans Bay. Under this luminous northern sky, distant Schoodic stands out bold and clear; miles beyond, the summit of Pigeon Hill appears, and Petit Manan lighthouse tower, entrance post to the Bay of Fundy, pricks the eastern horizon.

We close-haul our sails, round the black can buoy and glide out of the ocean swell into the smooth, sheltered anchorage of Bakers Island. Flood tide is only one hour old; and my quest is for fresh mussels in that clear, unpolluted water. We shoot into the wind, avoiding the numerous lobster-pot buoys, hand the jib and mainsail, drop the anchor and pay out scope on the cable. I pull the skiff alongside and row ashore. Spicy late summer fragrance wells out from the sundrenched island — sweet grasses, goldenrod, aster; even some of the white and pink *Rosa rugosa* for which this place is famous are still in bloom. The colorful sea bottom appears; gray sand studded with big smooth pebbles tumbled

and polished by millennia of winter gales, when the great
combers at high water rip over the reef barrier that now
makes this spot a sheltered harbor. Two more strokes of the
oars, and the skiff grounds on a rock; bucket in one hand
and boat painter in the other, I make a wobbly landing,
unlike the fishermen who splash boldly ashore in their rub-
ber boots. Mussels are there in great plenty, their dark blue
shells with brown "beards" clinging in clusters to barnacled
rocks and to the wooden ways laid years ago for the lighthouse keeper's skiff. In ten minutes' time I have gathered a
pailful, then shove the skiff off the rock where she grounded,
and row back to the yawl, facing forward to admire her
perfect proportions, and the backdrop of mountains.

We make sail once more, weigh anchor, and the yawl
pirouettes on her keel to head toward home. My young
sailor, blond and lithe as one imagines ancient Greek
sailors to have been in the Ægean, gazes, speechless, at
sea and mountains. What is he, at nineteen, thinking of
it all? Does the beauty of sunwashed shore and granite
mountains mean the same to him as to me, four times
his age? I respect the youth's right to his own thoughts
and do not ask, fearing perhaps to break the spell by some
offhand or discordant reply.

Now we close-haul the sails again to pass between Suttons
Island and the two Cranberries. I turn my back on the Isles-
ford shore where the summer houses are pretentiously in-
appropriate, but linger lovingly on the south shore of Suttons, its little cottages built in the good simple taste of a
century ago, when Maine men knew how to create as beautiful a house as a ship. Suttons, with its memories of John

Gilley and Mary Wheelwright, of picnics long ago, of clumps of blue harebell growing like weeds from the wild grass. In this bight of the Bay we encounter the inevitable spell of calm. The yawl holds her headway for two or three hundred yards, her sails full although the surface of the sea has become a wavy mirror; the ripples from her bows making sweet music. Finally her headway ceases, the sails gently flap, the booms swing from side to side, and the reef points play a tattoo on the mainsail.

What makes this particular day so memorable is its freedom from the mutter of motors. All power yachts are following the annual race in Blue Hill Bay, no snarling outboards are about. The lobstermen have finished hauling their traps and are at home eating supper. There is no sound but the lapping of waves on the shore, the lazy clang of Spurlings Ledge bell buoy, and the distant bark of a dog.

After a breathless calm of a quarter hour, the breeze returns, limp sheets stretch out taut with a clatter of blocks, sails fill, and the yawl heels to the last of the west wind.

Around the western point of Suttons, Bear Island makes

out. Its white lighthouse tower and pyramidical bell house seem to look down like benign parents on three tiny sloops that flutter past, having a little race of their own as they did not rate the big cruise. How many thousands of sailing craft have passsed that sea mark since 1839 when, at the suggestion of a naval captain, the government built the light station? How many seamen have blessed that winking white eye guiding them through Eastern or Western Way to the snug harbors within, or strained their ears to catch the deep-throated note of the fog bell?

Leaving the cliffs of Bear Island astern on the starboard quarter, we enter Northeast Harbor with the dying breeze, avoiding the ever present "Kimball's Calms" on the port hand. My boy lowers and neatly furls the jib, then stands with boat hook, poised like a classic harpooner, to spear the mooring buoy. Main and mizzen sheets are hauled flat to give the yawl one last graceful curvet before her way is checked in the wind's eye. Then the mooring rode is secured to the forward bitts, and the yacht's white wings are folded for the night.

IV. A SEPTEMBER CRUISE

THIS IS really my wife Priscilla's story; anyway, she is the heroine, and there's no hero. After hearing me read the previous chapter describing the beauties of a yacht's cabin and the delight of cruising *à deux*, she suggested that I write this as a warning to wives of sailormen that life on the ocean wave is not all fun and games.

This cruise from Northeast Harbor and back happened in mid-September 1956, in our 36-foot yawl *Emily Marshall*. I had just enjoyed a memorable all-male cruise to the St. John River, New Brunswick, and, with mistaken generosity, wished to share the delights of coastal cruising before the end of the season with Priscilla. Unlike New England girls, she was not brought up to sail. She is a beautiful and dainty Southerner from Baltimore, where girls are brought up to please men; but sailors (except the "middies" at Annapolis) seldom if ever crossed their horizon. She learned to ride and could "talk horses" with M.F.H.; she played a superlative game of tennis, and qualified as a professional musician; but "port" to her meant the wine that her father drank, and a "sheet" was something that you spread on a bed.

During the first five summers of our marriage, all was well between us on board the *Emily Marshall,* which I had had built after World War II for bachelor cruising. For Priscilla was gently initiated to the mysteries of the deep by my sailing master, Enos Verge of Thomaston, Maine. Enos was a sailor through and through. He had been brought up to sail fishing smacks and Friendship sloops, and then gone in for what he called "pleasurin'," i.e., yachting, as less arduous for a man approaching seventy. He was with Albert Harkness, Jr., William D. Stevens and myself in ketch *Mary Otis* when we sailed the latter part of the Harvard Columbus Expedition through the Bahamas and around Cuba; and on that voyage he showed such character, capacity and indefatigable cheerfulness that I persuaded him to take over the *Emily Marshall.* We were together for two summers before I married; but instead of resenting my taking to me a wife, as some sailing masters would have done, the first words that Enos addressed to Priscilla when she came on board were, "I'm so glad you married the Captain!" On that note he continued. Enos was always the perfect gentleman. He taught Priscilla in the kindest way the rudiments of steering and handling lines; he praised her cooking; he never disturbed our privacy; and he beguiled our days and evenings with tales of his adventures. And, whenever the weather looked doubtful, he gave me the hint to make port promptly, to spare Priscilla's feelings.

Most of our sailing with him was day sailing, but we three did have some delightful if uneventful cruises lasting two to five days. Had Enos lived, he might by his innate courtesy and gentle instruction have persuaded Priscilla to be more venturesome. But, alas, he was taken ill in the summer of 1953, and we had to send him first to hospital and then home; next spring he could only oversee the fitting-out of the yawl, and that summer he passed away to whatever heavenly mansion is reserved for the finest of sailors and the best of men.

There were no more Enoses to be found; his breed was almost extinct. So we made do every summer with a boy. Some were expert, others had to be taught even the rudiments of sailing, but none gave Priscilla much confidence. She was always afraid that I might fall overboard and the boy would be unable to maneuver the yawl to pick me up, since she probably could not have done it herself. Another trouble about the boys was that they had to leave around Labor Day for school or college. That was the situation in mid-September 1956. There had been several days of rainy weather, and when a clearing breeze from the north-west blew up, promising a stretch of fair-weather sailing, it seemed too good an opportunity to miss. So I proposed, and Priscilla accepted, to go on a short cruise with nobody but ourselves on board.

After topping off the fresh-water tanks and filling the ice-box, I brought the yawl under power to the float which we share with our neighbors. I moored her forward and aft, struck dunnage and provisions below, and made all plain sail, expecting to hand Priscilla on board and start immediately. But, in eagerness to be off, I mistakenly used old halyards for mooring lines instead of new, stout stuff, and compounded the error by belaying these lines to cleats on the float instead of leading them through rings back to the bitts on board, in which case I could have cast off from the yawl itself. Those mistakes would not have been serious had not a strong, puffy northwest wind been blowing directly down the harbor.

Priscilla tripped prettily down to the float, wearing her most becoming Gieves peajacket; with a charming smile remarked, "What a perfect day for a cruise!" and stepped gracefully on board. At the windward corner of the float I cast off the bow line, coiled it and flung it on board. At that very moment a strong puff of wind struck the sails, thrusting the yawl's bow away from the wharf; and just as I was running to the other corner of the float to cast off the stern line, it parted. In no time at all the yawl was six feet away and on the starboard tack, gathering speed; and I am no broad-jumper. A pretty fix for Priscilla, who wasn't supposed to know how to sail!

But she showed her breeding by keeping her head and using it, just as her grandfather Major Barton, on Stonewall Jackson's staff, had done at Chancellorsville. She followed her skipper's directions implicitly. First, I shouted to turn the wheel to starboard, to throw the yawl up into the wind and avoid our neighbor's small yacht moored nearby. Just before she was out of earshot, I again shouted, "Start the engine!" which, fortunately, she had learned to do; and, "Engage the clutch!" The yawl by that time had brought itself around on the port tack and was heading straight for the rocks. Following my arm directions — since, owing to the engine's noise and the wind, she couldn't hear a word I said

— Priscilla made a 180-degree turn; no easy task because the jigger was sheeted in close and the main sheet wound itself around the rudder post. It took all her strength to move the wheel. And, right in her way, was moored the great ocean-racing yawl *Ventura*. Priscilla afterward declared that *Ventura*'s crew boiled up from below, each carrying a deck mop to ward off the expected collision; but when I interviewed the sailing master after our return he said, "Oh, no, nothing like that; we saw she was doing all right. What a lady!"

As if *Ventura*'s presence were not bad enough, at that juncture, just as Priscilla was straining to clear the moored yacht, a motor cruiser conducted by one of the hopeless mutts who mishandle such craft, passed *between* her and *Ventura*, although it had the entire harbor in which to maneuver.

Having cleared *Ventura* and the stinkpot, with a strong wind astern and engine running, the yawl was really stepping out to sea. Priscilla afterward said that she felt she was headed straight for Lisbon, and that although she loved Lisbon, she didn't care to go there right then! I, in the meantime, was making circular arm gestures to head the yawl up into the wind toward the float, and that Priscilla did; all sails flapping, but the engine was strong enough to thrust the yawl to windward. When the yacht was a short distance from the float, I shouted to Priscilla to put the engine in neutral. And she, although shaking with apprehension, avoided bumping the corner of the float and made a perfect landing. I jumped on board, cleared the tangled sheets and again headed out of the harbor. Priscilla burst into tears of relief; and we decided to "splice the main brace." It was a remarkable performance, for she was "sick with terror" the whole time. It revealed her character, poise, and desire to save the ship; for she could easily have run the yawl onto the rocks near the float and jumped ashore.

What a start for a cruise intended to persuade a young wife that sailing alone with her husband was fun! But she never proposed to give up the cruise; that didn't cross her mind.

Since our destination was Blue Hill Bay, the fresh northwest to west wind forced us to beat to windward across Bass Harbor Bar and up the Bay, making short tacks inshore so as to take a look at the new cottages and camps. At about four-thirty we entered Sawyers Cove and shouted to the "Chubby" Grants, but they were out sailing in their new reverse-sheer *Controversy*. So we continued to the Watkinses' camp, fastened a line to their moored sloop, lowered our sails

and went ashore for a pleasant chat and cocktails with Gladys
and Bill. At six, when other guests began to assemble, we
returned on board, cast off, and motored into Prettymarsh
Harbor to anchor for the night. Then came supper of steak
broiled over the shipmate, potatoes boiled in sea water, lettuce salad and blueberry pie, accompanied by a bottle of
Beaujolais. Supper was followed by a good jorum of rum,
lemon juice and hot water while we discussed the events of
the day. Priscilla, after all her efforts, was in her sleeping bag
and fast asleep by eleven; I long stayed awake thinking over
my nautical sins of commission and omission. It was a beautiful, calm night in that quiet harbor; no other craft were
present, and no lights showed ashore except at the camps of
our friends.

The next two days were pure joy, as the weather was fine
and we didn't try to push things. With a fair wind we
threaded Bartletts Narrows and sailed between Newbury
Neck and Long Island into Blue Hill Harbor. It was almost
high water, so we were able to sail right up to the crumbling
wharves, go ashore and stroll through the village under the
hill — made famous by Mary Ellen Chase's *A Goodly Heri-*

tage. Blue Hill is a pretty village with a white-spired meetinghouse; but we wondered here, as elsewhere, why Maine villages always turn their backs (and backhouses) on their lovely harbors instead of welcoming the seafarer with shop fronts and restaurants, like Portofino and St. Tropez. Our own Northeast Harbor is perhaps the worst offender. The waterfront there looks like a secondhand car park. But in the near future it may at least have a few trees.

The tide will not let one tarry in Blue Hill's inner harbor; so, after making a few purchases, we dropped down to our favorite anchorage off the old steamboat wharf and enjoyed a second good supper and quiet night.

The third day, an offshore wind took us neatly down the bay past E. B. White's place on Allen's Cove where he writes those charming pieces about Maine for *The New Yorker*, past the now abandoned lighthouse off Flye Island and the entrance to Eggemoggin Reach, past the pretty spruce-clad islands that are called Merchants Row, down Jericho Bay and past Ringtown Island. We then entered Burnt Coat Harbor, Swans Island, rounding one of the prettiest lighthouses on the Maine coast. Burnt Coat, meaning that all the woods had been destroyed by fire, was the original name of the island when James Swan, a Boston speculator, bought it late in the eighteenth century and built a great mansion house which burned down over a century ago. But the rough old name has been kept for the harbor.

Burnt Coat is now a lobster emporium, and we stood up the harbor to anchor near a lobster car. When I put in there during World War II in Coast Guard cutter *Guinevere* (Captain Zachary Taylor Jones), the officers chipped in to buy every man on board a lobster; and for most of the sailors from far inland it was their first good lobster and a great treat. But the pharmacist's mate turned out to be allergic to lobster and thought that night he was going to die. Priscilla and I had a feast the night we spent at Burnt Coat, steaming the lobsters in a big pot with a scant two inches of seawater, as Enos Verge had taught us to do, and judging when they were done by another down-East trick — lifting the top lobster by one small claw; if he falls off, he's cooked.

We enjoyed a third quiet night, but the red dawn that followed was ominous, so I awoke Priscilla early, saying that we had better put away a good breakfast and get going. Heavy clouds were racing down from the north, the glass had dropped, and there was every evidence of an easterly gale making up. So, under power, we threaded the narrow easterly entrance to Burnt Coat Harbor, Priscilla washing up and making everything snug below. After passing The Sisters, we made sail. By this time the wind had veered to about due east, so we were able to fetch handily past Placentia Island — "Placench" as the local fishermen call it — and make Lopaus Point on Mount Desert Island. The tide was about half ebb, so I knew we would have a rough time getting over Bass Harbor Bar and suggested that we put into Bass Harbor and await a fair day to sail home. After a brief discussion we rejected the idea, remembering how we had dragged anchor right across that harbor the last time we put in there.

By the time we reached shallow Bass Harbor Bar, the combination of a force-8 easterly gale, and a 4-knot ebb tide (fortunately not a spring tide) running directly against it, had built up a nasty, short, curling chop. I started the engine and made for the channel buoy, with mainsail slatting wildly, dishes breaking below, and the wind screaming in the standing rigging. The yawl behaved magnificently, but the engine driving her into these steep seas forced her bows under each wave, and she was swept fore and aft. One big scoop of green water lifted off the forward hatch which I had neglected to secure from below, and away it went — I didn't dare turn back to recover. Another sea threatened to sweep the boathook and boom crotch off the cabin house, but Priscilla bravely squirmed up there on her tummy, and with water sloshing over her, secured both. She said later that crossing the bar frightened her less than the experience in Northeast Harbor; she trusted my seamanship and so felt better than when she was forced to go it alone. The crossing didn't bother me too much, as we were making good progress with the ebb and I knew that the rough water wouldn't last long. At the height of the excitement a lobster boat passed close aboard, headed for Bass Harbor; the skipper waved an arm and shouted encouragingly, "Two crazy people!"

As we emerged from the strong current approaching the gong buoy, the sea diminished sensibly; but the wind backed to east-northeast, heading us again. Knowing that we were in for another rough piece of water in the Western Way, and that the current would be against us there, I decided to use sail. Priscilla took the wheel and steered beautifully, although her heart was in her mouth since her man was up forward on the leaping deck, hoisting the jib. Once that was done, I stopped the engine, trimmed sheets, and away we went — making a good eight knots through the water, with lee rail awash but no more dollops of green water coming on board. That, to me, was the best part of the cruise; but Priscilla was praying that nothing would give way when we were so near "the haven where we would be."

As soon as Bear Island gave us a little protection I handed Priscilla the wheel, lowered and roughly furled the jib, flaked the main halyards for a quick dousing of the mainsail, and up into Northeast Harbor we sailed. By that time it had begun to rain hard and the harbor was popping like a bubbling cauldron with little spouts from the raindrops. Once more Priscilla took the wheel while we rounded into the wind, and again she steered perfectly so that I could catch our mooring buoy with the boathook that she had rescued. As soon as the warp was secured around the forward bitts, down came the mainsail, Priscilla inserting the salvaged boom crotch into its slot, seeing that the boom went into place, and hauling taut the main sheet to secure it. We then made a quick furl and handed the jigger in a jiffy. The dinghy, one-third full of water, was brought alongside and I rowed my thoroughly soaked but relieved heroine to the float whence she had begun her single-handed maneuver three days before.

When I told my French naval friends about "Priscilla's solo cruise," as I called it, they proposed to award her the decoration that used to be conferred on expert maintopmen in sailing ships; but, for me, the *Mérite Agricole,* the farmer's medal, for mooring with a rotten cable!

Not much of a cruise, some will say; you could have covered the whole of it with a fast motorboat in a few hours. But the experience, the sport of battling wind and waves; and, not least, the enhanced feeling for each other that emerged from all this, could never have been attained in any other way.

So, fainthearted wives, take courage from Priscilla!

V. THE ANCIENTS AND THE SEA

THE SEA has been a delight to me ever since I learned to pull an oar and tend a sheet, and sea literature has fascinated me ever since I began to read. Yet I should not have attempted this essay but for a verse in the *Odyssey* which was a great comfort during my labors on naval history in World War II. Odysseus, taunted by Euryalus in the Land of the Phæacians, replies, "Much have I endured in passing through this man's war, and the waves of the sea, laden with suffering."

That has been a recurrent motif in all sea literature, and the leading motif of the Greeks — "the waves of the sea, laden with suffering." The ancients accepted the sea as a source of daily bread and ready means of transport, but they were very wary of it. Never were they the "light-hearted

masters of the waves" as Matthew Arnold described them.
The Mediterranean, the only sea that they knew intimately,
is subject to sudden, fierce and dangerous storms; and such
poetry as the ancients based on their maritime experiences is
either tragic or cautionary, or expresses relief at reaching dry
land. They regarded the sea as a dangerous element upon
which they needed supernatural aid to prosper, even to sur-
vive. Sappho's lyric beginning, "I grow weary of the foreign
cities, the sea travel and the stranger peoples," is typical:

> So, a mariner, I long for land-fall, —
>   When a darker purple on the sea-rim,
> O'er the prow uplifted, shall be Lesbos
> And the gleaming towers of Mitylene.[1]

Nor did the sea enter their religion, except insofar as Poseidon and the sea nymphs could be invoked to protect poor
sailors plying their lawful occasions. The Middle Ages, on
the contrary, began to regard the sea as an element in or a
vehicle for religion; and only very recently, as history goes,
has man begun to look on the sea as romantic or as an element to sport with. Who ever heard of a Greek yacht, unless
a sumptuous row-galley on an inland lake? We have to wait
for sophisticated Catullus to find mention of a seagoing pleasure boat.

Aphrodite, loveliest of the Greek goddesses, arose from the
sea off a yet untroubled Cyprus. Greek mythology peopled
the sea with nymphs whose names represented its qualities
— Galēnē the calm and Glaukē the smooth; wave-swift Cym-

---

[1] *One Hundred Lyrics of Sappho,* translated by Bliss Carman (Boston: Page,
1904), p. 46. All other translations in this chapter are mine.

ythoë, rosy-armed Eunikē; Dynamenē the powerful, and swift-sailing Pherousa. These nymphs and fifty more are named by Hesiod in his *Theogony*.[2]

But Hesiod's view of the sea is very businesslike. He claims "no skill in seafaring nor in ships," and admits that his only sea passage lay across the Strait of Chalchis in order to take part in a song contest. "Such is all my experience of the many-fastened ships." Nevertheless, because the Muses have taught him to "sing in marvellous song," he will instruct his ne'er-do-well brother Perses in the profitable use of the sea. Two seasons of the year, he says, are best for seafaring: the first is "spring, when leaves on the topmost shoot of a fig tree are as big as a crow's foot. But I don't like it then; you will hardly avoid trouble." Early fall, "when the season of ener-vating heat has come to an end," is best; "for the winds then are steady and the sea is kind; but make haste to do your business and return home before the fierce southerly gales make up." And that is good advice for the Ægean, or even for the Gulf of Maine, today.

"Admire a small ship if you will," he tells brother Perses, "but stow your freight in a big one; for the greater the cargo, the greater your gain." In any case, "Leave most of your goods ashore and lade only the lesser part; for it is bad busi-ness to meet with disaster among the waves of the sea, and it is terrible to die among the waves."[3]

"Terrible to die among the waves." That note echoes all through Greek literature. If a sailor's body is washed ashore and given decent burial, that is not too bad — unless his

[2] Hesiod, *Homeric Hymns* (Loeb ed.), pp. 97–98.
[3] *Works and Days* (Loeb ed.), pp. 649–92.

grave is too near the sea. Here is a sailor's epitaph by Archias of Byzantium:

> Tho' shipwrecked, drowned and tossed ashore,
> I, Thēris, can't escape the ocean's roar.
> A stranger made my grave upon the verge
> Of mine old enemy; his deathless surge
> Beats alway on mine ear; I have no rest
> In this brine-drenchéd tomb. Hades were best![4]

Although the Ægean is subject to sudden and swift storms in summer, there is usually a long calm spell in the autumn. These were the halcyon days of the poets, when the kingfisher was said to build his nest on the surface of the sea. Apollonides bewails the loss of a friend whose ship at this calm season sprang a leak and went down: "When, tell me, Sea, shalt thou give safe passage to ships, if we must weep even in the halcyon days?"[5]

Homer's attitude is something else again. For him the sea was an element, not devoid of beauty, which a man must accept but should enjoy as best he may. In the *Odyssey* we find the sea endowed with poetic epithets that have echoed down the ages: *poluklustos,* the surging; *poluphloisbos* — loud-roaring; and *atrugetos,* untilled; *ēëroidēs,* streaked with the shadows of passing clouds. Yet, I wonder why Homer and the other Greeks did not find more color in the sea. *Oinops* (wine-dark) and *porphureos* (dark-gleaming) are very well for the hour of sundown when the Ægean turns a deep, reddish-purple like port wine; but Homer never, to my knowledge, alludes to the brilliant sapphire of the Ægean

4 *The Greek Anthology* (Loeb ed.), II, No. 278.
5 *Idem,* III, No. 271.

under a summer sun, or to the shades of green, reflecting the colors of the mountains, that it turns in the shallows near a beach.

Egocentric man loved the ships which he fashioned himself, before he came to love the sea on which they sailed. Homer was the first to admit it. His ships he calls well-masted, shapely; black (because their bottoms were pitched); red- or vermilion-cheeked because of the bright paint on their bows; well-benched because their primary motive power was the oar. And the description of her native city which he puts into the mouth of Nausicäa is as fair a one as you can find anywhere of a busy maritime community:

> Here the men are busied with the rigging of their black ships, with lines and sails and shaping the slender oar-blades. For the Phæacians care nought for bow and arrow, but for mast and oar and for the shapely ships, in which joyfully they cross the gray sea.[6]

6 *Odyssey*, vi.268–72.

To which Pallas Athene adds: "Trusting in the speed of
their swift ships, the Phæacians traverse the great gulf of the
sea"; and "their ships are swift as a bird on the wing, or as a
thought."[7]

In contrast to modern sea poetry, no ten lines of which can
a sailor read without discovering some landlubberly mistake
that offends him, Homer and the other ancients are very
careful to have their nautical technique correct. As an
example, take this description in the *Odyssey* (ii. 418–34) of
Telemachus setting sail from Ithaca, with Pallas Athene as a
distinguished passenger:

> The crew cast off the stern hawsers, stepped on board
> and sat them down on the oarsmen's thwarts. Athene
> of the gleaming eyes sent them a fair wind, a strong
> westerly that whistled over the wine-dark sea. Tele-
> machus now ordered his men to ship their oars and stand
> by to make sail, and they got the word. With lines of
> twisted ox-hide they raised the pine-wood mast, placed
> its heel in the tabernacle, secured it with the stays, and
> set the white sail. Now the wind filled the sail's belly
> and the waters parted, seething about the ship's stem as
> she roared ahead; and over the waves she raced on her
> destined course. Then, after they had nimbly made all
> lines fast in the swift black ship, the men brought up
> bowls brim-full of wine and poured libations to the
> deathless, immortal gods, especially to the daughter of
> Zeus, she of the gleaming eyes. Throughout the night
> and the following dawn the ship cleaved the ocean-way.

Here is a completely correct narrative of a vessel getting
under way, which would do for any yacht with a folding mast,

[7] *Idem,* vii.33–36.

substituting a "put-put" for the oarsmen to take her away from the dock out into a sweet west wind. But, alas, we have no Pallas Athene to send us a wind!

Homer's power to set a maritime scene in a few words is a never-failing joy. Take, for example, his description of making a landlocked harbor in Sicily, the land of the Cyclops. It has a beach where the ships may be drawn up, and a spring of sweet water that flows from beneath a cave. Here is how he describes Odysseus' fleet entering that harbor at night:

> In sailed we, and some god must have conned us through the heavy darkness, for the shore showed no light, and a low mist lay all about the ships; and *Selēnē*, the moon, cloud-covered, afforded no help from heaven. We missed the island at the entrance, and not until we ran our well-benched ships on the beach did we perceive the long swells rolling in. And when we ran the ships ashore we lowered the sails and on the verge of the sea we slept until the bright dawn.[8]

This passage in the *Odyssey* probably suggested to Vergil his description of a tiny landlocked harbor somewhere near Carthage, entered by Æneas:

> The harbor is made by an island whose outer coast breaks the great seas, so that only gentle swells surge within. As you enter, on either hand a cliff reaches up to the sky, and under their steep flanks the waters are calm and quiet. Low bushes, trembling in the breeze, grow upon the cliffs, and on their crests is a dark forest that casts a mysterious shadow over the water. Over against the island, under the overshadowing cliffs, is a little cove with a spring of sweet water and seats in the

8 *Idem,* ix.142–50.

living rock; the home of nymphs. Here the tired ships need neither cable nor sharp-fluked anchor.[9]

Most mariners will agree that Vergil has improved on his master. Many of us who have been around in small sailboats remember a tiny harbor that perfectly fits this description: Lombardo Cove in Acul Bay, Haiti, of which Christopher Columbus observed that you don't even need to anchor if you don't want to; Bunkers Cove between Great and Little Spruce Islands in eastern Maine, where I have spent a quiet night with anchor rode barely stretched taut while an easterly gale roared outside and the spruce trees on the cliff were literally trembling in the breeze.

Æschylus knew the sea at first hand better than any Greek poet except possibly Homer. In his *Agamemnon* there is a vivid description of the dawn over Tenedos: "When the beaming light of the sun arose, we beheld the Ægean flowering with the corpses of Achæans, and with flotsam from the ships." I am poignantly reminded of what one morning brought to view in Ironbottom Sound, Guadalcanal, in 1942. After a bloody night battle in which one of our cruisers went down, U.S.S. *Honolulu* steamed over the place where she sank, threading her way amid wreckage, corpses, and swimming sailors who waved and shouted, *"Honolulu! Honolulu!"* A young officer on the bridge reminded me how that sound echoed the "unearthly wail" (*thespesiē iachē*) from the spirits of departed warriors, wearing their bloodstained armor, which threw "pale fear" into the stout heart of Odysseus.[10]

[9] *Æneid*, i.159–69.
[10] *Odyssey*, xi.43.

Pleasanter images are invoked by another perfect phrase of Æschylus. He is describing the calm of a hot summer's day: — "The sea, all windless, sank to sleep upon her waveless noonday bed."[11] This recalls a summer in the Ægean when schooner *Ramah* in which I was cruising lay becalmed from dawn to dusk off the long, crested profile of Ikaria. We lay almost motionless on a gently palpitating sea, transparent as a vaporous emerald. Then a light westerly breeze sprang up out of the setting sun and wafted us gently through a starlit night to Patmos.

In his *Persians*, Æschylus has given us the classic description of a sea fight in which he took part — the Battle of Salamis. And I have no hesitation in asserting this to be the best story of a naval battle in all literature — a narrative ever memorable for the war cry of the Greeks, with its play on the noble word *eleutheria* — freedom: "O sons of Hellas, free your native land, free your children, your wives, the temples of your gods and the tombs of your ancestors!"[12]

Let us pause a moment on that word *eleutheria;* for the Greeks not only said it; they first practised it. Poignant as

11 *Agamemnon,* 565–6.
12 *Persians,* 400–3.

well as significant is the fable told by at least two Greek poets.
Xerxes, victor at Thermopylae, spreads a purple cloak over the
body of his vanquished enemy Leonidas, out of admiration
for his valor. The spirit of Leonidas, in the other world, re-
jects it; he wants no favor from the Persians. "But thou art
dead, Leonidas," says the poet; "why hate the Persians even
in death?" To which Leonidas answers, "The passion for
freedom dieth not."[13]

The Greeks had a word for everything, even submarine
warfare: *buthia naumachia;* literally, "deep-sea fighting."
Apollonides tells how Scyllos, the world's first submariner,
helped reduce the Persian fleet before Salamis and so helped
Themistocles to win; just as our own Pacific Fleet submarines
Albacore and *Cavalla,* by sinking two Japanese aircraft car-
riers before the Battle of the Philippine Sea, contributed to
that great victory.

> Scyllos, when Xerxes' mighty fleet
> Seemed sure to win, performed this feat: —
> Dove down — and this is true, not fable —
> Cut every Persian anchor cable.
> The ships, released, all drove ashore
> And Xerxes lost at least a score.
> Themistocles, you won the fight,
> But Scyllos helped you, that dark night![14]

Only when we reach the epigrammatists of the early Chris-
tian era do we find a note of play or pleasure in the Greek
literature of the sea. Antiphilos of Byzantium writes of the

---

13 *Greek Anthology*, III, No. 294.
14 *Idem*, No. 296. Cf. Pausanius *Description of Greece* X.19 (Loeb ed. IV
471), where he tells the full story, and how Scyllos was helped by his diving
daughter.

joys of cruising in a vessel much like the *kaikē* that one meets
in the Ægean today, with her high poop, waistcloths to keep
the deck dry, and firebox amidships for cooking:

> The topdeck of a sailing craft is where I like to lay,
> A-listening to the weather-cloths resounding from the spray;
> A pot upon the fire-stones with briskly bubbling noise,
> And chow served up by any one of sundry unwashed boys.
> While sailors talk and "roll the bones" on some convenient plank —
> With simple mariners like these I'm always hale and frank.[15]

A Greek bawdy-house keeper once built a ship out of his
profits. This appealed to the Hellenic sense of humor, and
more than one epigrammatist tried his hand with the theme.
Here is a part of Antiphilos's effort, though I can't produce
all the play on words; *phukos,* for instance, meaning both
seaweed and the paint used by courtesans. The ship speaks:

> Let Cypris view me, land-begot, a'roaming o'er the sea;
> My rig befits a saucy gal of sportin' company.
> Fine linen I can spread aloft, and pretty paint below,
> As on my mother's element I travel to and fro.
> Come, all ye hearty mariners, come mount me by the stern;
> So long as you can ply an oar, free passage you may earn![16]

From these quips of the epigrammatists, let us run the
gamut of Greek literature in the first century A.D. to the
New Testament. There is no better story of a stormy voyage
in antiquity than St. Paul's, as related in the Acts of the
Apostles, chapter xxvii; but the translation in the King James
version is such as to suggest that Paul was no sailor, or that
the apostolic narrator told it wrong. So, about a century ago,
a classically educated master mariner of Boston, Captain John

---

[15] *Greek Anthology*, III, No. 546.
[16] *Idem*, No. 415.

Codman, undertook a new nautical translation of this chapter to prove the contrary.[17] It is such a delightful bit of salty prose that I shall quote a few verses:

8. Hauling upon a taut bowline so that we just passed to windward of it, we ran into Fair Haven, not far from Lasea.

9. Now, d'ye see, we had made a long voyage of it altogether, and as it looked squally ahead and there were signs of bad weather, Paul called all hands aft, and says he: —

10. "Shipmates, this looks like a bad business; and if we keep on it looks to me as if this ship and cargo will come to grief, and maybe we'll lose the number of our mess."

11. Now, getting under the lee of Clauda, we had hard work to get alongside the boat we had been towing.

17. But they finally hoisted her up to the davits and passed a belly-lashing around the old ship to thrap her together. And then we got out of the shoal water, having clewed up and furled everything, and let her run before it under bare poles.

18. Coming on to blow harder and a heavy sea on next day, they hove overboard some of the cargo.

19. Next twenty-four hours coming in hard gales and sea increasing, all hands and passengers turned to and hove overboard all the gear lying about decks.

20. Weather so thick that we could not get a meridian altitude of the sun nor a lunar observation for several days. Gale still continuing.

21. In the mean time Paul had not given any more

17 S. E. Morison "Captain Codman on the Mutiny in Dorchester Church, and the Seamanship of St. Paul," *American Neptune*, (April 1942), II, 99–106.

advice, but now he called the officers together on the poop and said, "Well, gentlemen, you had better have taken my advice and laid quietly at anchor in Crete, and then it would not have been a case of general average.

22. Keep a stiff upper lip, and believe me now when I tell you that whatever may happen to the ship, all hands will be saved.

23. For the Angel of the Lord stood alongside of my bunk tonight,

24. And said, 'Don't be afraid. You are bound to get to Caesar, and on your account the whole crew and all the passengers shall be taken care of.'

25. So, gentlemen, don't give up the ship yet, for I believe the Lord will do as he said."

By and large, the Greeks felt that the best thing about a sea voyage was the harbor at the end. And the Romans were no different, Catullus and Vergil excepted. Typical of their attitude is Seneca's remark to the effect that a few miles' sail along the Italian coast was so "tedious and dreadful" that he'd rather take twenty years to make a journey by land than make another sea voyage. Catullus wrote the only known poem of antiquity to a pleasure boat, his *phasellus*. Like a modern yachtsman, he boasts of her as the speediest of vessels — *navium celerrimus;* none afloat could beat her, whether under oars or under sail; and she has sailed all waters between the Euxine, where she was built from a leafy forest on Mount Cytorius, to the windy Adriatic. He loves her so that when she became too frail for the sea he had her hauled up to his villa on Lake Como, where she sits out her old age ashore and makes her prayers to Castor and Pollux.

Sir Richard Livingstone, in a letter to me, expressed his doubt whether Vergil really cared for the sea; but "he had to say something about it," having to bring Æneas from Troy to the Tiber. "And he shows that precise observation which is one of his most obvious gifts. . . . You must have often seen the sea by moonlight as it is described in *Æneid* vii.8–9." That was after Pious Æneas had made sail and left the harbor:

> *Aspirant aurae in noctem, nec candida cursus*
> *luna negat, splendet tremulo sub lumine pontus.*

The night breezes blow; the bright moon refuseth not to illuminate the voyage, and the sea is resplendent under her trembling light.

Vergil tells of seamen watching the weather from the beach where their ships are drawn up, and the light breath of Auster, the south wind, inviting them to set sail.[18] And of the sea on an ironbound coast, in words that convey even the sound of surf crashing against cliffs:

> *et gemitum ingentem pelagi pulsataque saxa.*[19]
> And the mighty roar of the sea and the battered rocks.

Palinurus, Æneas' weather-wise pilot, rises in the night and, like a modern sailor, turns his face this way and that to feel the direction of the soft night airs. He observes the stars silently sailing their courses through the heavens: — "Arcturus and the rainy Hyades, and the two Bears," and

18 *Æneid, iii.*70.
19 *Idem,* iii.555.

Orion "armed and belted with gold."[20] When he is satisfied
that the heavens portend fair weather, he mounts the quarterdeck and summons the Trojans in words that ring like a
bugle call:

> *dat clarum e puppi signum; nos castra movemus.*

> He gives the clear signal from the poop, and we break camp.

They spread the wings of their sails and resume their voyage.
All night they roar across the Ionian Sea. Then Vergil gives
us the finest record in all literature of the way a sailor's heart
leaps up at making a long-desired landfall: —

> *Iamque rubescebat stellis Aurora fugatis*
> *cum procul obscuros collis humilemque videmus*
> *Italiam. "Italiam!" primus conclamat Achates,*
> *"Italiam!" laeto socii clamore salutant.*

> And now Aurora blushes red among the fading stars, when
> afar we make out faint hills and low-lying Italy. "Italy!" first
> sings out Achates: "Italy!" repeat my shipmates with joyful
> shouts.[21]

Now father Anchises breaks out a great bowl, fills it with
wine and, erect on the quarterdeck, invokes the gods:

> *Di, maris et terrae tempestatumque potentes*
> *ferte viam vento facilem et spirate secundi.*[22]

> Ye gods of the sea and the land, lords of the wind and the
> tempests, Grant us good passage we pray, send us fair breezes
> to follow!

On sped the Trojan fleet, and Rome was founded.

---

20 *Æneid,* iii.514–17.
21 *Idem,* 521–24.
22 *Idem,* 528–29.

To conclude, there is nothing in all maritime poetry, in my opinion, comparable to Vergil's, with the exception of his great imitator — or some will say, improver — Dante Alighieri. *The Divine Comedy* includes some of the best sea poetry ever written. In the eighth book of the *Purgatorio* he gives marvelous expression to that feeling you have at the beginning of a long and uncertain voyage under sail, first day out, when night falls and sea and wind make up, and you wonder why you ever left your comfortable quarters ashore:

> Now comes the hour that turneth back desire
>   from seamen bold, and melteth every heart
>   when from sweet friends and home they must retire.
> And the new pilgrim feels the selfsame smart
>   when on his hearing tollèd bells implore
>   the day which dying from him doth depart.

Dante's high point, for a lover of the sea, is his account in Book XXVI of the *Inferno* of Ulysses' last voyage. Dante is listening to the shade of Ulysses, the aged seafarer who came to grief because he would take just one more cruise:

> So I set sail upon the purple sea
>   in one light pinnace, with that selfsame band
>   who faithful were through all my fortunes low.
> As far as Spain we saw on either hand
>   the lofty shore, Morocco, and the flow
>   of sea round Sarde and many an island base;
> I and my shipmates ancient were and slow.
>   When we bore in upon that tidal race
>   where Hercules his pillars set abreast,
> "Brothers," said I, "who with me, face to face
>   through myriad dangers have attained this West;
>   and now remains but half a seaman's vigil

Of all that's left of life's unceasing quest,
    will ye refuse for fear of further peril
    westward the world unpeopled to explore?
Think ye your mothers had for nought their travail?
    'Twas men, not brutish beasts their wombs once bore —
    men, born to virtue and intelligence!"
When this they heard, my shipmates roundly swore
    they'd follow me to death — my eloquence
    had cured them of all wish to stay ashore.
Now swung our stern on morn's magnificence,
    and ashen oars made wings for our mad flight
    onward and onward, steering south-southwest.
The stars antipodean ruled the night,
    and homely constellations sank to rest
    below the ocean's rim, beyond our sight.
Since we had entered waters deep and clean,
    five times the moonlight had the ocean dressed,
    and five times stripped of all her silver sheen,
when there appeared to us a mountain, blue
    with distance, one so great I'd never seen;
    the seamen shouted as they caught the view.
But soon their merry cheers were turned to wailing
    when off the new-found land a whirlwind blew
    straight on our barque, and over us prevailing,
thrice whirled her helpless amid angry waves,
    tossed up her stern, the rudder unavailing,
    pressed down her bows, as pleasèd Him who saves —
until the sea closed over us again.

Herein Dante, as only a great poet could, penetrates the soul of the eternal sailor, who can never bear to stay ashore as long as he has a ship, and willing shipmates to share the danger and the ecstasy of rolling over the multitudinous seas "laden with suffering," if you will, but refreshing the soul of man as nothing else, short of religion, can do. And Dante, too, predicted the forthcoming age of discovery. For it was seamen, imbued like Ulysses with the spirit of adventure, who in sailing craft discovered America, who reached the uttermost recesses of the seagirt land; and now in aircraft fly over it from pole to pole and girdle it under water in nuclear-powered submarines.

VI. A SUMMER CRUISE IN THE ÆGEAN

A DREAM of my boyhood was realized in 1934. Some thirty
years earlier, studying Greek history at school, I traced
in my *Atlas Antiquus* imaginary routes among the islands of
the Ægean, and sailed in fancy the circle of the Cyclades.
And I waited to visit Greece until I could do so by sea, as the
ancients did; in a sailing vessel that can go anywhere, whose
smooth motion is in harmony with the sounds of wind and
waves; whose white wings make symmetry with mountains,
native lateeners, and the "multitudinous sea incarnadine"
— Homer as seen through Shakespeare.

My old friend and shipmate Dr. Alexander Forbes made

the dream come true, and his medium was the schooner
Ramah of Boston. She was a sturdy, able vessel, 100 feet over
all, Nova Scotia–built and Gloucester-fisherman design, long
black hull and graceful sheer and lofty masts. Her sail plan
consisted of a whacking great gaff-headed mainsail that
needed two stout fellows on either halyard, a gaff-headed
foresail, jumbo, jib, jib topsail, and fisherman staysail. No
troublesome genoas with their clacking winches, no bellying
spinnaker, no brasswork, brightwork or other yachting re-
finements; all inside ballast and an old-fashioned back-
breaker windlass that never jammed or slipped. *Ramah* was
built by Columbus Iselin for his oceanographic work; Dr.
Forbes installed an auxiliary engine and refitted her for a
surveying expedition to northern Labrador, and after that
was accomplished, sailed her in the summer of 1933 from
Gloucester to Naples with an amateur crew. Having been
designed for Arctic rather than Ægean conditions, *Ramah*
was stuffy below; but that did not bother us, for everyone
slept on deck under the stars. Not a drop of rain fell during
our six weeks' cruise, although often there was a gathering
over the mountains of clouds that to Yankee eyes looked like
thunderheads. And only one of the dozen nights we spent
at sea was sufficiently rough to bring spray over *Ramah's*
stout bulwarks. That night was a tough one; and before we
were through, she was stripped to reefed foresail. Small
native boats sail the Ægean constantly; but they know the
signs and stay in port when a norther is making up.

Our auxiliary engine was not strictly necessary, but highly
desirable for making schedule in the limited time at our dis-
posal. We had about the same proportion of light, baffling

airs and calms that dog yachtsmen in Long Island Sound in
August. But more often there blew a brisk nor'wester that
whipped up whitecaps and sent *Ramah* along at eight or nine
knots. The wind almost always died away to a gentle zephyr
at night, when *Ramah* would ghost along, making no sound
except the slap of vang and topping lift against the mainsail.

The Ægean is so beautiful that I would gladly cruise it in
any old sailing craft. But the ideal boat would be an auxiliary yawl or schooner, not less than forty or more than a hundred feet long, with flush decks, plenty of skylights and
well-fitting awnings, a kerosene stove, large fresh-water tanks,
and a good ice chest. Our electric refrigerator used up so
much power that Dr. Forbes scrapped it at Naples and built
in a roomy old-fashioned icebox which we found means of
replenishing in every seaport. We were not troubled by the
heat at sea, only ashore at midday, so easily fell into the
Levantine habit of taking a siesta after lunch.

A pair of shorts and sandals and a sun hat formed the usual
male costume on board; ditto for the girls, plus one of those
handkerchief arrangements that tie around the neck. Wendy
Morison, Kitty Forbes and Janet Forbes made as lovely modern replicas of Hera, Aphrodite and Athene as one could find
anywhere; and little Florrie Forbes, piping on a clarinet, became our god Pan. Her eleven-year-old brother Irving, who
has since become head of the music department at Exeter,
made more mischief than music on board *Ramah*, but he and
all the rest joined the girls in song. Sundown, in those
waters, is the time to clap on something extra, although the
air is deceptively balmy all night; the natives, we observed,

were never without a woolen bellyband, and some of us who
tried near-nudism for the whole twenty-four hours regretted
it.

The crew were all amateurs, chosen with an eye to work
as well as friendship. There were five young Harvardians,
including the handsome athlete-poet John Cotton Walcott
who was killed in World War II; one from Princeton, and
Pascoe, son of Dr. Grenfell of Labrador fame. At Cos, the
Italian authorities objected to the girls' being entered on our
yacht's papers as "stewardesses," the point being that as "passengers" they could have been taxed. They threatened to
keep our documents until we paid up. So we put on a show
for them. One morning all men and boys went below; the
four girls made sail and weighed anchor with an occasional
assist from their mothers, but none from the men and
boys. Upon returning to port that evening, our impounded
ship's papers were courteously returned and no more was
said about taxes. The Italians were so impressed that the
story of this exploit preceded us to Rhodes, where a friend
seeking news of us was asked, "You mean the yacht sailed by
a crew of pretty girls?"

My rating on board *Ramah* is best described as that of the
ancient *mystagogus,* guide and initiator to the mysteries. I
was supposed to sell Hellenic culture to the youngsters, who,
belonging to a generation deprived of its intellectual heritage, a sound classical education, knew next to nothing of
Greek history or literature. But some of them, who had
studied under the late George Harold Edgell, were better
versed than me in Greek art. Almost every day on board I
read aloud for an hour or two from translations of Greek

authors relevant to places in our itinerary, or the works of Zimmern and Livingstone. Theocritus and Herodotus were the favorites; the one portrays the rural life that we saw in the islands, still going on very much as in the fourth century B.C.; and in the historian's pages we followed the progress of Xerxes' army and fleet to its disasters at Platæa and Mycale. What a grand old fellow Herodotus was! Far from being the uncritical raconteur that many have asserted, he writes with the most subtle art, bringing out the characters of individuals and places. And he never forgets what so many modern historians never learn, that history is primarily a story of mankind; not economics, sociology, or wisecrackery.

Alexander Forbes, owner and skipper of *Ramah,* and at the age of fifty-two the oldest person on board, is a truly remarkable character and one of the most versatile men of our era. Like the other Forbeses of Milton and Naushon, he has sailed a boat since childhood, and become an expert navigator. Trained at the Harvard Medical School, he became a physiologist by profession, and his discoveries on the working of human muscles have gained him high honors in America and England. An inventor too, he helped install radio direction finders in our destroyers in the first world war, and as commander U.S. Naval Reserve in the second world war he provided some new devices for the military photographers. As dead-reckoning and celestial navigator he is quicker and more accurate than most younger men in working out a position. An explorer, he had already surveyed and charted northern Labrador in *Ramah.* At the age of sixty, he was chosen by the Army Air Force to reconnoiter, and later to help set up, air bases like "Crystal One" in northern Labrador, to expedite the transfer of fighter planes from the United States and Canada to the United Kingdom.[1]

Alex is still a familiar figure on the ski slopes of New England, figure-skating on the rinks, and on board his yacht in any harbor you can name between Long Island Sound and the Labrador. To the age of eighty he piloted his own plane, in which he and his charming wife Charlotte flew to meetings of the several learned and professional societies of which he is a fellow. A philanthropist, Forbes for years has been the good angel of the George Junior Republic, and has unobtrusively helped many young men to obtain an education. He has a fine and very special sense of humor, and is an excellent raconteur. A grandson of Ralph Waldo Emerson, he has inherited the features and in no small part the character of the Sage of Concord. On board *Ramah,* following his example, there was none of the bellowing, swearing and bawling-out that take the joy out of so many yachting cruises, although first mate Roger Hallowell occasionally transmitted some of the skipper's quiet orders in the sharp bark which earned him the nickname "Woof." It was typical of Dr. Forbes that, after we had incurred considerable expense for repairs after grounding in the Little Dardanelles, he said, "Sam, do you think I ought to ask the insurance company to pay for this, since it was all my fault?" He did not lose his temper even when importunate muleteers, seeking his patronage at Santorin, knocked a camera out of his hands. After this cruise I said, and after another thirty years I repeat, that Alexander Forbes is the best all-round shipmate and the most

[1] Described in his book *Quest for a Northern Air Route* (Cambridge: Harvard University Press, 1953).

Christlike character I have ever known, whether layman or cleric.

The one paid hand in our ship's company of seventeen was the cook, Antonio Francesco of Naples. Although he was supposed to be trilingual, his Greek was entirely expressed by signs, and his English was limited to, "dirty Greeks," "fry-'em-up-eggs," "galley damn hot," and "finish." This last word came out when we tacked unexpectedly in a stiff breeze. The icebox door flew open and the contents fetched up on Francesco, on the lee side of the galley. When discovered fighting off a quarter of lamb, a bowl of cold marcaroni, two quarts of milk, several dozen eggs and a mass of broken crockery, he remarked with great emphasis, "Feenish!" But he didn't finish, and was soon combing the egg out of his hair and cheerfully preparing the next meal. His culinary repertoire was limited to what he had learned in the Italian merchant marine. This appeared at our first breakfast on board. Hoping to order something easy, Bessie Morison, the only person on board who could speak Italian, ordered boiled eggs. Francesco threw four dozen eggs into a cauldron of cold water, brought them to a boil, and boiled them for an hour. Bessie suggested that, next time, he bring the water to a boil, drop in the eggs — here Francesco interrupted, "If you do that they go *pouf!*" throwing up his hands to imitate an explosion. Possibly the grade of eggs issued to the Italian merchant marine did just that, but ours were of somewhat superior quality. Nevertheless, Francesco could not soft-boil eggs properly, so "fry-'em-up-eggs" became the daily breakfast dish. His spaghetti, however, was the real stuff; his soups and stews were excellent. Like all cooks in this part of the world,

Francesco preferred to buy poultry on the hoof, and had a die-hard cockerel on board who called the morning watch on deck with a lusty crow. At Patras, as we lay alongside the quay, a woman with a bamboo pole drove a score of docile turkey hens along the water's edge, dodging horse, donkey and auto traffic. At a word from her the flock halted and the herdswoman snatched up a couple of likely turkeys by the legs and displayed their good qualities to Francesco. At Piraeus he traded in some empty bottles and oil tins for a canary bird, whose cage hung from the main boom while in port.

We were not altogether dependent on Francesco's culinary art. All Greek seaports except Athens are oriented to the waterfront, and the best restaurant is apt to be a few yards from the anchorage. While our chain was rattling out of the hawsepipe, the waiters would rush a bevy of tables to the edge of the quay and make signs to us that food and drink were awaiting us ashore. We often fell for them, and found Greek cooking excellent. Aristophanes reminds us that Euripides' mother sold pot-herbs for a living; and a skillful use of herbs still gives Greek food a peculiar flavor and zest.

There were many interesting dishes, new to us, such as a
miniature squash the size of a gherkin, strange little fish,
delicious when sautéed with herbs; sherbets made with the
juice of fresh peach, apricot or melon. And such melons as
are grown in the Argive plain, and the rocky island of
Cephalonia, made every other kind seem insipid. The prize
dish in Greece is a Turkish heritage called — *Iman biali,*
meaning "the Iman fainted" (presumably from joy). It is
eggplant cooked up with tomatoes, onions, almonds, half a
dozen herbs, and served cold with olive oil.

The wine is even better than the food. Greece produces
several hundred varieties, from the humble *retsinata* which
tastes like spruce gum (and explains why Dionysus sports a
pine cone on his thyrsus), to the red, fruity *malvoisie,* the
malmsey of medieval England, in a butt of which a certain
Duke of Clarence met a pleasant if dishonorable death.
Every island has its own vintages; none without some virtue,
and most of them good and incredibly cheap. After a pleasant hour of wine-tasting at Herakleion with my newly ac-
quired friend George Polychronides, I had a five-gallon jug
filled with a sound, well-aged, white Cretan wine for the sum
of $1.60. Near Patras they make a respectable imitation of
champagne that retails for forty-five cents a quart. All this
was highly informing to our young people, brought up under
prohibition, who imagined that there were only four or five
varieties of wine in the world. It took me most of the voyage
to dissuade them from applying the name sherry to *mavro-
daphne,* port to the black wine of Santorin, and so forth. A
Greek listener-in to one of my impassioned harangues on the
subject asked if I were an American wine merchant! If so,

I would specialize in the Achæan vintages, which travel better than the others and several of which can be had in the United States.

Traveling by sail, in your own home as it were, is easy and comfortable in Greece; much better than cramped motoring, with the problem of a new hotel at the end of each day. It is true that in most European countries there are more regulations for vessels than for cars; but not in Greece. At Argostoli in Cephalonia, our first Greek port, we paid $5 for a compulsory month's pilot dues, although we never used a pilot; since it is one of the principles of Skipper Forbes that the surest way to run aground in a strange harbor is to accept local advice. A sound principle, too, for what is "12-foot draft" to a Greek pilot? He instinctively thinks of his shoal-draft lateeners. Wherever there is a town and a customhouse, the ship's papers have to be shown; but except at Piraeus there are no harbor dues beyond a few cents for a stamp. And everywhere, as we land, some returned Greek-American greets one with, "Hey, boys, how's Boston?" and helps one to answer the numerous friendly questions that the captain of the port asks of strange yachtsmen.

It was different, however, when we left the jurisdiction of Greece and began sailing among the lovely Dodecanese, the twelve Ægean islands occupied by Italy between the two world wars. There the officials were legion, the regulations meticulous, and the dues relatively high. There was trouble, too, when we re-entered Italy at Messina. Since Mussolini was then picking on Greece, the local authorities insisted that, having lately come from that presumably dangerous country, we must undergo a quarantine of several days or a week. Dr. Forbes's eloquence (supported by a letter from his classmate Franklin D. Roosevelt) and Francesco's assurance that we had never, never mingled with "dirty Greeks" finally enabled *Ramah* to proceed toward her destination in Naples. We were not allowed to purchase fuel, which had run out; but it didn't matter, the winds were more prosperous than they had been to Ulysses, and we romped safely under sail between Scylla and Charybdis. Scylla, incidentally, is now a straggling town, which according to our cook contained not one honest man; and Charybdis is a very feeble whirlpool, a mere whiffle on the water. Something must have happened since Ulysses' day to reduce it; or Ulysses, like so many sailors, was a liar.

To our great regret we were unable to land in Asia Minor, for the Turks in 1934 were in a highly suspicious humor toward foreigners. Even with a Turkish visa we would have had to visit Smyrna to obtain a permit to touch at any part of King Croesus' ancient kingdom. So we had to be content with a telescopic view of the white marble castle at Budrun, the ancient Halicarnassus. One day, while rounding the lighthouse at the tip of the Bybassian Chersonese and passing within a quarter mile of the site of ancient Cnidus, deserted and as yet unexcavated by Turk or Giaour, some of our young men were for going ashore to see what they could pick up; but elderly prudence forbade. A few days earlier, as we subsequently learned, two British naval officers swimming from a cutter near the Turkish shore were shot at by a sentry, and one was killed. It was all a tragic mistake. The Turks beckoned to the British to approach for examination, but they turned the other way; for the Turks beckon with the palm of the hand toward you, so, naturally, the British thought they were being ordered to sheer off, and the sentry fired to stop them.

Bathing is delicious in the Ægean, and we were in and out of the water several times a day. One was sensible of the greater saltiness compared with the Atlantic. The color is a sapphire blue under the summer sun, turning smaragdine in the shoals, and in a calm, reflecting all the colors of the mountains. Toward nightfall it turns deep purple, the wine-dark of Homer, not the incarnadine of Shakespeare. Bottom is often visible at ten fathoms. We missed the tides of our New England coast, and the variety that they give the shore-line. With a rise and fall of but a foot or two, there is no scope for seaweed, clams or mussels to flourish; and the hard line where earth meets sea has the monotonous regularity of a lake shore. But raise the eyes above that, and you find a mountain landscape hard to match anywhere. Some of the mountain slopes hung heavy with vineyards, terraced corn-fields where the red-ocher earth was breathing after the summer harvest and before the fall planting. Other slopes were planted with olive, each tree having its own retaining wall and morsel of earth. Still others were all gray rock and scrub, affording pasturage only to goats; and in some places there were cliffs gay with color as those of Martha's Vineyard. Almost all the flowers had gone to seed, and pineclad slopes were rare; but one soon learns to ignore detail, or even color, and to look for form and mass. For pure form, the Greek mountains are as completely satisfactory to the eye as Monad-nock is to a Yankee; one feels that they are what mountains should be. No long even ridges or bizarre pinnacles, but hills molded by an unseen artist into noble shapes. Greek mountains are always varied, never monotonous; every few miles they part to admit a valley with bright green vineyards, gray-green olive groves, and often a bright little town of white, blue-trimmed houses, ending in a tiny quay with a fleet of lateener fishing boats. Under our skipper's expert navigation it became one of our greatest pleasures to feel the way with leadline after dark into some nameless valley cove, anchoring as soon as the leadsman cried, "By the mark, five!" and awakening to the tune of goat bells in a new scene of Arcadian beauty. We did this at Voudia Bay in Melos, and at several other harbors that are not even named on the Admiralty chart.

The original Arcady is the center of the Peloponnesus; and right well does it deserve to have given a name to idyllic existence in romantic scenery. We approached it from Nauplia, a lively little town at the head of one of the world's loveliest bays. Two days we spent exploring Mycenae and the fertile Argive plain; then chartered a motorcar and drove through the heart of Arcady into Laconia and Lacedaemon. It was a drive of spectacular ups and downs, with comparatively level stretches in valleys. In classical times each of these miniature mountain-walled plains was an independent city-state, normally at war with the next valley; too fiercely nationalistic to unite with its neighbors, safe for a brief moment against the Persian. What a preview Greek history is of our twentieth-century world!

Through the long Tegean plain sped our car: long stretches of wheat and barley stubble pastured by sheep and goats, tended by white-kilted shepherds in jaunty red leather shoes. Circular stone floors where the grain is threshed with flails or trodden out by the hoofs of oxen. A brief halt in Tripolis, the busy market town of Arcadia, then upward past terrace after terrace of tiny cornfields to the divide, where the only vegetation was scrub oak; then down the broad valley of the Eurotas, facing mighty Taygetus, guardian of Lacedaemon.

We had been to Athens and wished to visit the site of her stern rival, although little there is to recall Sparta but her site, as Thucydides predicted. The deserted Byzantine town of Mistra, on the slope of Taygetus, offered more of interest than the ruins of Sparta, once the terror of Greece. But her defeated rival Athens still lives through the deathless glory of her intellectual and artistic achievements. Indeed it was for these that she was chosen the capital of modern Greece, and has become once more a great and populous city. It may be well for Americans to reflect that arts and letters go on paying material dividends to a country long after business has cracked and liberty vanished.

Not that Athens neglected the manly virtues: we had a spectacular illustration of that on our approach. With mainsail and jib-topsail set, we beat against a refreshing easterly from Eleusis through the Strait of Salamis, site of the naval battle in which Greece, under Athenian leadership, saved Europe. There was the site of Xerxes' ringside seat, and all the familiar land and seamarks that we had read of in Herodotus' prose, and in the poetry of Æschylus, himself a combatant. After clipping the waves where the fight had been thickest on that September day 2400 years ago, we emerged into the Gulf of Ægina and there, sweeping the

Attic coast with marine glasses, caught Athene's rock and the glorious Parthenon. Before that immortal and perfect monument the modern city faded into nothing. And as we swung into the wind and dropped anchor in Phaleron Bay at sunset, Athens for us put on her violet crown.

As I look back on the cruise, it seems studded with rare moments when present beauty, past association and congenial shipmates struck the contrapuntal harmony that one finds in a composer such as Brahms. There was the morning in the Gulf of Corinth when dawn over Parnassus conjured out of the night a mountain amphitheater around an ocean orches-

tra, on which the quickening land breeze played, shoving our
lee rail awash. There was another cool morning off Cape
Sunium, when the sun rose from the Ægean and kindled the
frosty white columns of Poseidon's temple to pure gold, and
we landed from the schooner's dory on the ancient stone
slipway built for biremes and viewed the temple with nobody
else about but Greek goatherds. They, eager to please their
unexpected visitors, plucked big leaves and rolled them into
cornucopias, into which they milked a complaisant nanny,
and proffered us the doubtful refreshment of warm, fresh
goat's milk. There was an evening when we watched the

sun-god sink into the sea from his own Mount Cynthos, over-looking his island birthplace of Delos, the slope from summit to water's edge paved with ancient marble. There was an afternoon when we lay becalmed under Ikaria, stretching along the glassy sea like a giant sea-monster and breeding clouds from her lofty back. The engine was not working, the ice had melted, and there was no more bread or butter on board; but we spread an awning over the main boom and relaxed, and at nightfall a gentle breeze made up and wafted us to Patmos.

The Ægean was not a sea empty of all but pleasure craft, like our New England coast today, but full of little native traders, *kaikēs* or caiques as they are called, lateen or fore-and-aft rigged, their topsides painted vermilion and other gay colors like that "saucy girl" in the *Greek Anthology.* Cos, with the ruined temple of Æsculapius an appropriate place of pilgrimage for our skipper; the ancient monastery at Patmos, commemorating the cave where St. John the Divine received his Revelation. The approach by sea to Lindos on Rhodes, with its acropolis of the pre-Christian era, is magnificent, and the old Byzantine town clustering about it, of surpassing interest.

In Rhodes there were glimpses of rural life such as Theocritus described in his seventh Idyll: shepherds resting with their flocks by a spring, a smell of ripening figs in the air, cicadas creaking and chattering in the olive trees, and a day owl hooting musically. An evening walk along Mirabella Bay in Crete, while the mountains turned from gold to deepest purple and the music of goat bells accompanied our march. Nights at sea, greeting friends like the Pleiades and

Hyades, and Spica and Vega, in the country where Hesiod wrote about them 2700 years ago. Peaceful nights at anchor, when a light movement of the waters set the topmasts tracing arabesques among the stars at zenith.

In six weeks' cruising in these waters, where none of us were acquainted with local conditions — and at that time there were only three buoys in all Greece — we had but one mishap; a gentle grounding in the Little Dardanelles, when an inshore current during the calm before sunrise carried us off our proper course. But *Ramah* was soon lightered off, the damage was repaired at Patras, and the cruise continued to Naples. That the Ægean can be very nasty at times we learn in sundry books from Homer's day to ours, and from what we experienced on that rough night north of Crete. For St. Paul's seamanship I have a much greater respect than before visiting the scene of his voyage. But hundreds of American and European yachtsmen have cruised in the Ægean with no serious trouble. You need not wait to be the fortunate owner of a big schooner like *Ramah* to sail Greek waters.

When the cruise was over, I wrote in my journal, "I intend to return, and in any sort of sailing craft; for there are still several routes traced out by my schoolboy pencil in the *Atlas Antiquus* that *Ramah* had no time to follow." Thirty years have passed and never have I been able to return, although yearly George Polychronides, my friend at Herakleion, begs me to come back. Pursuit of Columbus sent me to the Caribbean, and the Navy in World War II took me to the Pacific. In both seas one may find scenery comparable to the best in Greece; but Hellas enhances her present beauty by the writings of those imperishable writers and artists who once dwelt there, and the memory of St. Paul who threaded the islands in a sailing vessel and addressed the "men of Athens" from the Areopagus.